BLUEBERRY MOON

THE

POEMS & APHORISMS

OF

KIM LEE SEAGULL

Kim Lee Seagull

FERNHOLM PUBLISHING

BLUEBERRY MOON

THE POEMS & APHORISMS OF KIM LEE SEAGULL

FERNHOLM PUBLISHING
Post Offiice. Box 89
Winfield MO, 63389-0089 U.S.A.
Orders @fernholmpublilshing.com

All rights reserved. No part of this book may be reproduced in any form or by any means, electronic or mechanical, including photocopying, recording or by any information storage and retrieval system without the permission from the author, except for the inclusion of brief quotations in a review.

Copyright © 2011 by Kim Lee Seagull

First edition: ISBN: 10: 1-883165-72-5
               ISBN: 13: 978-1-883165-72-7
Printed in the United States of America

Cover and book design by June Helen Fleming

Library of Congress Catalog card Number: 2010938385

Publisher's Cataloging-in-Publication
(Provided by Quality Books, Inc.)

Seagull, Kim Lee.
   Blueberry moon : the poems & aphorisms of Kim Lee
Seagull. -- 1st ed.
   p. cm.
   Includes bibliographical references.
   LCCN 2010938385
   ISBN-13: 978-1-883165-72-7
   ISBN-10: 1-883165-72-5

   I. Title.

PS3619.E254B58 2011   811'.6
                                QBI10-600223

TABLE OF CONTENTS

THE POEMS

1. BASS LAKE
2. LADY OF THE MOON
3. MAY YOUR BEST PERCEIVE ME
4. THIS SINGULAR INNOCENCE
5. PLATO, THEY NEVER PLAYED OR LOVED AS I HAVE CHOSE
6. YOU ARE THE CAROL
7. THE WOE TO BE ALONE
8. WHILE WAITING FOR A LUCID LASS
9. I LOVE YOUR KIND AND PRETTY WAY
10. THERE IS A RUMOR ON THE WIND
11. HOW I LONGED FOR YOU
12. WHEN I NOW RECALL
13. A GIFT OF SPANISH PEARLS
14. FROM A TETHERED GOLDEN EAGLE
15. WONDERFUL WOMAN
16. TO A CERTAIN WOMAN

17	SHOULD YOU AVOID ME MORE
18	TO MY DEAR MOM
19	YOU RESTORED MY HOPE
20	WHERE IS MEANING BOLD
21	TO MY DEAR MENTOR
23	TO AN AMAZING OLD FRIEND
24	TO THE FIRST LADY
26	MAJESTIC RAPTOR
27	NATURE IS DEDUCTIVE
28	TO NATIVE AMERICANS
29	THIS IS LOVE
30	MY PRAYER FOR YOUR SON
31	AFTER THINKING ON PLATO'S REPUBLIC
32	SONSHINE
33	THE BIRTH OF THE SUN GOD
34	THE SUN OF HEAVEN WITH THE GLORIOUS MANDATE OF HEAVEN
35	THE SUN OF RIGHTEOUSNESS - ELIJAH REPAIRS THE WORLD
36	DIVINE INTERVENTION
37	TO THE MAJESTIC GOLDEN EAGLE

38	COURTSHIIP FLIGHT OF THE GOLDEN EAGLE
39	THE CANADIAN SNOWBIRD
40	ON TRANSCENDENTALISM AND THE REALM OF GOD
41	DEDICATED TO: SCIENTISTS, POETS AND MADMEN
42	MISSOURI MORNING - TWO BELOW ZERO
43	THE SECRET OF THE GOLDEN FLOWER
45	THE PROPHET AND THE DISTINCTION BETWEEN EMPIRICAL GENIUS AND TRANSCENDENTAL GENIUS

THE APHORISMS

53	WITH MUCH AFFECTION
54	THE SECRET OF DESIRE
55	PASHA LARA - MY WHITE GERMAN SHEPHERD
56	THE LOGIC OF LOVE
57	THE VIRTUE OF LOVE
58	LOVE
59	THE BURNING DESIRE FOR LOVE
60	THE CELIBATE SAGE
61	TO EMILY DICKINSON - A FANTASY

62	THE LONELY BED OF WINTER
63	MY DEAR OGDEN
64	YOU LEFT ME
65	BUG
66	A FACT OF LIFE FOR SOME
67	SELF-DESTRUCTION
68	THE CAREFUL PATH
69	LIBERATION
70	HEMINGWAY
71	SOL INVICTUS - THE UNCONQUERED SUN
72	TO NATURAL BORN WORLD SHAKERS
73	THE WISE
74	WHAT THE BUDDHA TAUGHT
75	A MODERN ZENIC WAY OF TEA
76	THE PARADOX OF ZEN
77	WISDOM FROM THE DHAMMAPADA ON SELF-CONSTRUCTION
78	THE GLORIOUS PATH
79	ENLIGHTENMENT
80	WISDOM FROM WISDOM TRADITIONS
81	A MYSTIC'S VIRTUE, AND THE INVISIBLE LABOR OF THOUGHT

82	THUNDERBIRD
83	THE ATMAN
84	FAME
85	I PLAY DICE WITH THE WORLD
86	CHAOS THEORY IN PRACTICE
87	PHILOSOPHIES GREATEST CONCEPT
88	A MYSTICAL INSIGHT
89	ON PHYSICS AND FRIENDSHIP
90	CREATION FROM THE NOTHING THAT DIDN'T EXIST
91	UNIVERSAL INTERCONNECTEDNESS
92	THE REASON WHY NO EMPIRICAL FORMULA CAN MEASURE LOVE
93	THE HARMONY OF NATURE AND THE LAWS OF PHYSICS
94	CON-SCIENCE
95	SPIRITUALISM
96	TO POETS
97	ON THE SOURCE OF POETRY
98	ON THE GREATNESS OF POETRY
99	SONGS
100	MYSTICAL POETRY
101	AN INDIAN FAREWELL

102 THE CAUSE OF SO MUCH SUFFERING

103 CHILD ABUSE

104 WHAT THEY CANNOT KNOW

105 EMPATHIC ANALOGY

106 I AM CERTAIN

107 TO THE POLICE, THE FIREMEN, AND THE MILITARY

108 MY BLESSING FOR YOU

THE ESSAY

111 THE MYSTICAL REFUTATION OF THE GRAND DESIGN

POETRY DEDICATIONS

6 - TO CAMILE CARROLL

7 - TO MY DEAR DIANE HALDANE

8 - TO KAREN MASTERS

9 - TO MY DEAR CRYSTAL THOMPSON

10 - TO MY DEAR DIANE HALDANE

11 - TO MY DEAR PATTY HARRIS

12 - TO MY DEAR DIANE HALDANE

13 - TO NANCY

14 - TO STACIA MOTTA

19 - TO DR. GARRY M. VICKAR

20 - TO MOTHER TERESA

21 - TO AMBASSADOR DR. ANANDA W.P. GURUGE VICE PRESIDENT OF THE WORLD FELLOWSHIP OF BUDDHISTS

23 - TO PRASERT RUANGSKUL THE HONORARY SECRETARY-GENERAL OF THE WORLD FELLOWSHIP OF BUDDHISTS

24 - TO SECRETARY OF STATE HILLARY RODHAM CLINTON

26 - TO PRESIDENT BILL CLINTON

27 - TO REVEREND DR. JOHN POLKINGHORNE WITH MUCH ESTEEM

THE LOGICAL PARADIGM

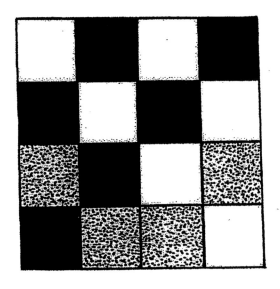

DEDICATIONS

For my Mom and Dad
Are these words,
A poet might
'Ve had!

Garry Vickar
Francisco Garriga
Kevin & Joanne Gordon
Karen Daubert & Bill Hubbard
Neil Diamond
Richard Bach
Kris Kristofferson
The Moody Blues
Elvis Presley
Bob Dylan
The Eagles
The Beatles
Josh Groban
Andrea Bocelli
Melissa Manchester
Judy Collins
Crystal Gayle
Celine Dion
Sara Evans
Anne Murray

All you guys choke me up
Just Like the Holy Spirit!!

ABOUT THE AUTHOR

I was born in the beautiful town of Haileybury, Ontario, Canada, now called Temiskaming Shores. I visit my homeland often because I love the magical land, of my childhood! It was in Haileybury, where I had my first mystical experience, as a child.

My dear grade five teacher, Peggy Hammerstrom, had a powerful influence on me. She had us memorize 100 lines of poetry for the year, and it became one of the best experiences of my life, because I developed a great love for poetry.

When I was ten-years-old, Canada challenged public school students to draw a fire prevention poster, in a national contest. I drew a great bull Moose struggling through a burnt out forest, with his great head hung low in sorrow. I decided to call it, "He Once Was King." It was chosen as one of the top ten posters in Canada!

I am also a portrait artist, working in the 19th Century style, known as "stippled drawing." The entire image, takes months to do, in tiny dots of India Ink.

I chose the pseudonym Kim Lee Seagull because my favorite story, Jonathan Livingston Seagull by Richard Bach, was made into a motion picture, and by a transcendental coincidence, the soundtrack was composed, and performed by my favorite singer songwriter, Neil Diamond, and he gives me a tingling rush, when I hear him perform.

I do indeed hope, that you will discover a poem, or an aphorism, in this collection that you like.

BLUEBERRY MOON

THE POEMS

BASS LAKE

It was in the moon
Of ripe Blueberries
When the great Gulls
Shed their feathers
That she came like
The prayers of morning
At this sacred time
And in this holy place
The yellow Buttercups
Grew fervent
And the Devil's Paintbrush
Was everywhere
It was here among
These flowers of summer
That I asked the
Wild Daisies
If she loves me
Oh – Oh my Soul
If only my count
Was mistaken –
She loves me not

LADY OF THE MOON

Oh Lady of the Moon
So special is your gift
To put my heart in tune
With the universal drift.

Oh soft and tender light,
Oh gentle glowing sphere,
Do brighten up my night
In answer to me here.

May Moonlight always rest
In these eyes mooring,
Until She is the quest
Of sunlight in the morning!

MAY YOUR BEST PERCEIVE ME

May your best perceive me
And your judgment bear
The words won't deceive you,
Because they're true I swear.

They mark without dispute,
The awesome measure of repose
That my heart could not refute,
Unless itself dare it oppose;

For in the tingling spell
Of our first proximity,
My heartbeat rose and fell
From both ends of infinity!

THIS SINGULAR INNOCENCE

The Universe exploded from a Singularity
Gas and dust formed the firmament
And radiant galaxies whirled in the void
Like grand rotating Ferris Wheels
All kinetic – formed by God's immortal love
So why are my starry eyes shy before you
You – the tender object of my shine
I cannot stare upon your ethereal form
Reputed by all to be sublime
Even the dog of a gentle master
Knows the tremendous danger of a stare
For lust without affection is a prison for the soul
But true love liberates the spirit's fire
For the libido is weaker than affection
Oh woman – you have my heart ablaze
I faint before the sweet words come out
Of these trembling lips of love
Born from the unspoken rapture
Of this Singular Innocence

PLATO, THEY NEVER PLAYED OR LOVED AS I HAVE CHOSE

They never played or loved as I have chose
Nor was I falsely led to their repose
Or welcome some emotion's sweet affect
For one's beauty whose love I would select
And what I'd do to lie with her by night
Who dazzles with her bosom beauty bright
Though this childish heart within my breast
It beats as though it were a lost conquest
The other whose spirit outshines the rose
That climbs the arbor but by none is chose
Which God her fragrance gave a sweeter power
And leads me to this wilted little flower
She claimed herself from God a Mystic's birth
And then became a Form in Heaven on earth

YOU ARE THE CAROL

You are the carroll
In this happy heart;
My force to fare all
Lest your song depart.

For with your kind devotion,
Mere words become an art
From the manic motion,
Here in a poet's heart.

So fate it is for you,
My dear to always stay
In this poor poet's verse,
Long after we are clay!

THE WOE TO BE ALONE

That Genius from beyond
Lent my heart reprieve,
Since He more than fond,
Did so artfully conceive.

His favor fashioned well
A beauty that is breathless,
And doubtless I can tell
That's why my heart is restless.

But paradox is rare
To marvel at and moan,
The love she may not share,
Oh the woe to be alone.

WHILE WAITING FOR A LUCID LASS

While waiting for a lucid lass,
Fate forbad my discontent;
In but a moments pass,
Her course was my way bent.

I watched with an ecstatic eye,
The lass the Lord had sent;
The rapture I alone espied,
Did in my heart ferment.

Oh woman where you stand,
So nigh your fair aspect,
When I ask you, take my hand,
And please do, my love accept!

I LOVE YOUR KIND AND PRETTY WAY

I love your kind and pretty way,
And the sweet whisper of your voice.
Like the dawning of a perfect day,
You are the golden girl of choice.

With those kind eyes and winsome smile,
Girl you cause all the joy in me;
So hold this moment for a while,
And perhaps God will let it be.

THERE IS A RUMOR ON THE WIND

There is a rumor on the wind
Breaking the silence of the shore
Where Seagulls glide and cry
Friendship's communal lore

A kind of echo from below
A burden only to the air
Resounding off the cliffs above
The great sound of Gulls below

I have seen them come
And I have seen them go
But the joy that brings them back
Is friendship don't you know

HOW I LONGED FOR YOU

When the soft Spring wind
Blew my long hair about
And the first Robin
Had finally returned home
My dear how I longed for you

WHEN I NOW RECALL

When I now recall
How happy I was then
It was how tenderly
You filled my mind

A GIFT OF SPANISH PEARLS

I possess such attraction
To the beauty of your form
There is no distraction
To which I will conform

My love a plenitude
Assumed no danger there
Where upon your gratitude
Would count this love as rare

Could I rearrange the Zodiac
So our horoscopes discern
Spanish Pearls against the sky
And our stars our love confirm

FROM A TETHERED GOLDEN EAGLE

Your ideas grandly reported
Burn creatively in me
With all idleness aborted
Such wonders set me free

You make a treat of thought
Worth unbounded thinking
Flaming fiery hot
And mind illuminating

Your genius cut my tether
My imagination has no bounds
Our dear friendship together
Has turned my life around

WONDERFUL WOMAN

Wonderful woman, I must say,
Your mind, so perfectly refined,
Must have caused Him great delay;
For He so carefully designed,

And your shape that He devised,
Marks the measures took
To stagger nature-lover's eyes,
When they are blessed a look.

With body matched to mind,
How more perfect could you be?
And God is more than kind
To share a sense or two of thee.

So I am slave to your wish,
But the freedom I can't bear
To wait on it is anguish,
Wondering if your wish I'd hear.

Oh my soul, should your demand
Bind that which you require,
Before it, naught would stand,
If my wish were your desire!

TO A CERTAIN WOMAN

It's certain I know a woman,
That none other can compare.
She may be just a woman,
With virtue more than a share;

For, attracted the stranger's eye
Will follow her here and there,
With less respect than I,
To disturb her with a stare.

And welcome is her beauty,
To snare the passion spent,
And render as its duty
The heart to quick content.

I did prudently suppose
That she alone must view,
So by poem I did disclose
That she my friend is you.

SHOULD YOU AVOID ME MORE

Should you avoid me more
Than that which I can bear,
Then only poems will store,
The love I could not share.

And that which fate might not,
To me your best bequeath,
Would leave me just the stars,
To marvel at beneath.

So try to think now of
What words have not withheld,
Am I just to love,
That which cannot be held?

TO MY DEAR MOM

I marvel at your soul
So sweet and so sublime
I wish I could extol
In verse your loving mind

You are like a flower
That blooms above the snow
A transcendental power
That only God and mystics know

He gave you a tender spirit
And a mind of radiant light
That brightens your bright virtue
Beyond my gift to write

YOU RESTORED MY HOPE

Even the darkest night
Can't prevent the dawn
Even the boldest lie
Can't obscure the truth
And even the complex universe
Couldn't confuse an Einstein
Like all these wonderful things
Even the extreme anxiety
Of my tortured mind
Was little challenge
For the power you possess
To restore hope in my life
And rebuild this happiness

WHERE IS MEANING BOLD

Where is meaning bold,
When nature's tune is vile
With all its laws to hold,
The sentence without trial?

On this I have wondered,
More than I had wit
And have my life considered
In trade for ken of it.

But so fond of you am I,
That if the answer writ
Were in the range of eye,
I 'd fain see you than it!

TO MY DEAR MENTOR

Ananda as I write
Empowered by love
I'm lifted like a Golden Eagle
On friendship's wings
Beyond all emotion
Where hope is infinite
Beautiful and free
And this poem is crafted
From my heart to thee

Ananda you inspire me
With your clever mind
And gentle heart
Like a great sage
The world is better
Because you are here

The Middle Path
On which you tread
Belongs to all
That want to win
The Buddha's peace
You help us all
By your example

Ananda I believe
You guide me
Like a father
Does his son
Like a mother
Tending to her young

Think upon this now
However you must
And know the truth
That on some
Great day hence
I'll be a better man
Because of you

TO AN AMAZING OLD FRIEND

My mind moves upon
Your mental emanation,
Like lyrics to a song
Worth the contemplation.

So sing to me your best,
This lover of your wisdom
And I need not attest
To another religion:

For Mara is my strife
And you, a Flake of Snow.
I can endure the life,
Where Crystals of Glory grow!

TO THE FIRST LADY

In what dearly dreamed verse
Composed by this poet's hand
Could command the words to write
Upon the First Lady of this Land

She bears a lawyer's logic
And knowing sanctions bounds
Can undermine the caustic
Courtroom battlegrounds

She has enormous stature
Born of wisdoms grand decree
The resonating rapture
Of regard for you and me

She would never order the arrest
Of some simple homeless man
Or mock those politicians
That are like a charlatan

She has a remarkable dignity
And conducts herself with pride
Beyond the arrogant way
Of those that can't confide

She can lift the people's spirit
Merely by her presents there
Without a conscious effort
It'd be something to be there

She moves the people's hearts
Like the trees by the wind
And when they depart
Very few would rescind

And she leaves you struck with wonder
At her tenderhearted way
Just like the rain and the thunder
Dispelled by the light of day

January 14, 2000

MAJESTIC RAPTOR

You soar on Majestic Raptor's wings
Through the corridors of power
Like Philosopher Kings
Bald Eagle of justice your love shall portend
The Red Dawn of liberty for Native women and men
Now the American Indian will call you friend
Mattaponi - Nez Perce - Cheyenne - Arapaho and Sioux
Talons of power to name but a few
Could become true sovereign Nations because of you
So will this Eagle Nation now respect the Red few
Or Native People shall dread a distant age
That one day may dawn so darkly without you

NATURE IS DEDUCTIVE

I don't know why the laws of nature
Take the form that they do, but
I do know why we can discover
Them through mathematical
Insight. Mathematical insight is
Deductive reasoning, and nature
Itself is deductive. That is why
Scientists can discover the laws
Of nature; those laws are deductive
Like the laws of mathematics.

TO NATIVE AMERICANS

Please dear God bless our
Magnificent Indian Peoples
The poorest of the poor
Here in America's shame
The richest nation on earth

THIS IS LOVE

Nothing can stir the spirit
To loftier heights
Than the realization
That there are others
More valuable than ourselves
This is the center
Of true religiousness
This is love
As the ego loses its power
Over our faculties
We necessarily displace
Our love from ourselves
Outward into the world
Trusting that our love
Will Catch someone
With a prayer

MY PRAYER FOR YOUR SON

Should your son be granted
A plain and gentle mind,
Then he needs no standard
Aside conventions' kind.

But if his mind is kindled
With love's burning seed,
Then let his life is mingled
With the poet's breed;

For cause affects their virtue
To bear the truth as boon,
When there is no church to
Make the poet room!

AFTER THINKING ON PLATO'S REPUBLIC

When I discontent with self-ignorance,
Left amidst the black canvassed sky,
I questioned from within, the stars at chance.
They tell me not - left with why?

Curse you demon devils, curse you!
Tease me as the magnet at a pin.
Destitute this heaven's earth I see,
Find me then content in hell's sin.

Ah but for my sullen thoughts and state,
Dear Lord leave me not; pity me,
As I have cursed my own fate.

Though for me a virtue Lord you sought!
In haste for ken as Philosopher-Kings,
I'd beckon hell half knowing things!

SONSHINE

I never saw the Sun
As well as here from Troy,
Or the stars from Haileybury,
Where I was a little boy.

Had I the way to do it,
I'd rise and set in Troy,
Then wander north at night
To see the starlit sky.

THE BIRTH OF THE SUN GOD

Love is the Morning Star
Tummy-blushing with her Son
That Bumblebee Avatar
Stung them sweet as one

Be Bumblebeatification
From the Daystar's sacred pen
Do tell with rhyme and reason
The Dawning of Aten

Oh sweet honey dripping Sun
How golden is your birth
Sol make all people one
And conquer hell on earth

TO THE SUN OF HEAVEN
WITH THE GLORIOUS MANDATE OF HEAVEN

With brilliance of Sun
And modesty of dew,
What artist has hung
A more perfect hue?

What poet in praise
Has marked in a line,
Your unnatural ways
Of being sublime?

Did He not mourn
For the ignorance in man,
So that He would form
A more mystical man!

THE SUN OF RIGHTEOUSNESS
ELIJAH REPAIRS THE WORLD

He was the worshiped Light
When Heaven gave him birth
The I Ching his Consecration
Gave him power on the earth

So what affect upon our world
Will Malachi's Sun god be
The Christ he's come to herald
For all the world to see

He cried his name Elijah
And worked for world peace
Before Christ the Messiah
Returns to the Middle East.

DIVINE INTERVENTION

In all my time, I've hardly spent
A happy moment, knowing well I could
Succeed unhindered in calm content;
For when the mood is bound to serve me good,
And action knows no counter cause,
I'm thwarted by a damnable condition,
Which seeks to undermine creative laws;
By the test for plays, I won't audition.
Though act I could, I'd rather write the play.
The play'd be good, as good a play can be;
Though they may try to see the worst and say:
His luck is surely serendipitous.
As long as wit has luck, the truth may be
As clear as glass, through which the eyes can see.

TO MY MAJESTIC GOLDEN EAGLE

On majestic wings of ecstasy
With talon's clenched in Love,
We are Golden Eagles tumbling
From a thousand feet above.

I'm mystical with passion
How could I let you be?
This noble verse I fashioned
Is just meant for you and me.

Your beauty stirs my heart,
Your proud eyes set me free,
Oh how I wonder all the time
Why you gave your love to me.

COURTSHIP FLIGHT OF THE GOLDEN EAGLE

Round and round
This courtship flight
From three thousand
Clear blue feet,
In an elaborate aerial
Display of amorous intent,
The regal blue-blood male
Circles wide above his choice.
Then suddenly swoops down
Toward her as she
Rocks this lover's dance,
Flipping on her back
Beneath his awesome lust
Her noble feathered feet
With talons opened skyward
To trap her single choice.
Their razor claws clutch together
As they tumble coupled in ecstasy
Crashing toward the ground
Until lust of their minds
Breaks in a climactic release.
Then apart they fly with
This life-long bond
Of love confirmed.

THE CANADIAN SNOWBIRD

In a careful methodical way
In order to protect or to shield his people
From the manic rage of a Golden Eagle
The anxious Cherokee Eagle slayer
Upon his Great return to the Tribe
Wisely proclaimed that he had killed
A Snowbird and not an Eagle
The tiny Snowbird being too insignificant
To be dreaded by his people

ON TRANSCENDENTALISM AND THE REALM OF GOD

I
The brain is the matter
And the Mind is the Form

II
The rapture of reason
And the Absolute Idea

III
The mystical intuition
And the Ecstasy of Love

IV
The genius of the Atman
With the Godhead above

DEDICATED TO: SCIENTISTS, POETS AND MADMEN

Since the form I underlie
Is all I can behold,
Whereabouts in it am I,
Whom lifeless atoms mold?

Am I just the order,
That animates the form?
Me within this border
Where thoughtless atoms storm!

Had this occurred to you,
As urgently to me;
Then perhaps our atoms flew
On path-o-logically!

MISSOURI MORNING - TWO BELOW ZERO

Have you seen the gray
Of oaks in wintertime,
Or the frost of February
On the window pane?

Have you seen the deer,
Struggle through the yard
Near the start of year,
When the living's hard?

Or the grape so Holy
Stuck up through the snow,
Like the sacred oak
That will insist to grow.

THE SECRET OF THE GOLDEN FLOWER

Oh what did you see
In that glorious Golden Flower
What may that secret be
That only wisdom knows the power

I tingled with delight
Degraded not to mirth
By knowing from its sight
My own transfigured birth

One too may know the world
Through meditation's doors
And be the one to herald
The way to Heaven's Shores

So Buddha where you stand
Explain to me the power
And point me to that land
Of the Golden Flower

Then let me see more clearly
And help me to discern
The way I can austerely
Find the path of no return

Notice when you tingle
For love causes that to be
That my son will point you
To the sacred Bodhi Tree

Feel the weight of the world
Lift like a mystic's shroud
Modesty has you exalted
For Heaven resists the proud

Oh Master - oh Master
I've Bodhisattva power
No - Nirvana - no Nirvana
I'm returning like the Flower

THE PROPHET AND THE DISTINCTION BETWEEN EMPIRICAL GENIUS AND TRANSCENDENTAL GENIUS

There are two realms. One is the realm of nature,
And the other is the Transcendent Realm of God,
And the Platonic Forms, and Ideas. God does not
Exist because that implies that God is either
In the universe somewhere, or God is the body
Of the universe, which Spinoza called pantheism,
A belief that Albert Einstein loved so much.
However, God is transcendent from this
Commonplace world of nature. No scientist
Will ever discover God in the universe.
Perhaps a way to describe the Transcendent
Realm is the Zero-Dimension, or the Prevoid.
Before the four-dimensional space-time
Continuum - Einstein's concept - the Zero-
Dimension, or Prevoid is neither somethingness
Nor is it nothingness! It is Isness, because
God Is! The absolute, Transcendent Realm
Always was. It was before the universe
Came to be, and will be after all the stars
Are dead! This divine presence of God
Always was and forever shall be,
Because it is the Godhead.

The transitory, commonplace world we live in
Is the realm that the empirical genius can
Understand, and therefore describe, because
Nature is deductive, like mathematics.
But the only one that can comprehend and
Describe the Transcendent Realm of God,
Is the transcendental genius. The greatest
Empirical genius will never be able to
Measure love, because love is Transcendental!

It is the transcendental genius, the mystic -
With the majestic, manic heart - that can
Describe, or approximate the true
Measure and worth of love, in poetry,
And all of the world's religious scriptures.

The most eminent empirical genius can
Logically see the beautiful paradigm in
Empirical data, and - one day - generalize
It into a simple, elegant all-embracing
Mathematical model, or Universal Theory
Of Everything, like all the most brilliant
Theoretical physicists talk about.
A grand perfect universal earning its
Place in the absolute Realm of Platonic Forms.
Such is the wonderment of mathematics!
Because nature is deductive - like the
Deductive, aspect or nature of mathematics -
Mathematics can symbolically, positively
Correlate with, and therefore perfectly mimic,
Or model nature's deterministic macrocosm.
This is not true in nature's microcosm of
Subatomic particles where non-linear
Chaotic events can only be understood
In terms of probability and chance.

The transcendental genius can mystically
See the Realm of god in a grain of sand,
Like William Blake, a wild flower like
Tennyson, or a snowflake, like Francis
Thompson, and he can best describe it
With poetry. Poetry is the supreme,

Intuitive, mystical language of the
Transcendent Realm; it is the analogue
Of mathematics, the supreme logical,
Deductive language of nature.
Between the transcendental mystic
And the empirical scientist, the
Mystic is the grander of the two,
For only the mystic can truly enter
The mystical Realm of mystery and
Wonder! All truly great mystics are
Poets, just as all truly great physicists
Are mathematicians. Of course, we
Very much need both kinds of genius,
The empirical and the transcendental.

The sacred pathway by which one can
Realize the mystical nature is to
Experience enlightenment. The way
The mystic can tell that he is
Enlightened is by the big sore lump
In his throat, and the tingling rush
In his body when he perceives
Something worthy of veneration, and
Therefore great in life. This is a
Tingling apprehension of goodness,
And it is the prerequisite of his
Greatness, and proof of his lofty soul.
The more he tingles the more enlightened
He is, and only he can tell; for none may
Know it just as he may. He will never
Tingle from something evil. This
Thrilling sensation and the big sore lump

In his throat are the momentous
Movements of the Holy Spirit! It is the
Will of God guiding him! It is God's
Greatest gift of spiritual Enlightenment!

God guides the most virtuous and
Innocent mystics by Transcendental
Coincidence. It occurs where the earthly
Realm and the Transcendent Realm
Coincide or meet in mystical contact,
In the ecstatic mind of the mystic.
When that occurs, then the mystical
Poet - in the grandeur of his ecstasy -
Can mysteriously learn the will of God.
It is that gift from God that empowers
The mystical poet, granting him more
Power than a king! When that happens
The mystical poet becomes godlike,
Like a god, a liberating god like
Ralph Waldo Emerson had in mind!
Now, like Confucius, he possesses
The Mandate of Heaven, and should
Become an acknowledged legislator
Of the world by counseling world
Leaders, something Percy Shelley
Would approve! By the infinite grace
Of God the mystical poet can, in
Tranquil contemplation, use divination
Devices to play dice with the world,
Something Einstein would not approve
Of, because he said, "God does not
Play dice with the universe." The

Holy divination devices may have
Been similar in practice to the casting
Of lots, as it was done in the New
Testament era, seeking providence
By chance, or like the long lost
Urim and Thummim, described in
The Hebrew Bible to consult God.
It could even be like the holy I Ching used by
Confucius in ancient China, to consult the
Transcendent Realm of Heaven. This was done
For expedience, rather than wait for seemingly
Random Transcendental Coincidences.
By experiencing these sacred, holy
Transcendental gifts, one becomes one
With the will of God. One becomes a prophet!

BLUEBERRY MOON

THE APHORISMS

WITH MUCH AFFECTION

To Garry M. Vickar, MD
Who helped me pick
My tether -
And set me
Free!

THE SECRET OF DESIRE

Desire is a form of
Selfishness in the
Common man,
But it is a divine tool
In the mind of a sage,
Because he desires the
Happiness of others too.

PASHA LARA - MY WHITE GERMAN SHEPHERD

I'm covered with the hair
Of the Dog that loves me.

THE LOGIC OF LOVE

Hate's end
Is love's beginning!

THE VIRTUE OF LOVE

Love is not baffling
For even a child
Can understand it

LOVE

Love is Transcendental

THE BURNING DESIRE FOR LOVE

I can't blow out
The flame of desire,
But that which I desire,
Is itself holy!

THE CELIBATE SAGE

Something living touched me.
It was only a fly.
Thank God you touched me.
Even the stinging bee loves me!

TO EMILY DICKINSON - A FANTASY

The bees are drunk
On the nectar
From the flowers
Of our love.

THE LONELY BED OF WINTER

The long night
Is cold and dark
A blizzard rages on
The great buck
Is crying for his doe
While here on my bed
I sleep alone

MY DEAR OGDEN

Can the humble Seagull
Ever be the noble Eagle

YOU LEFT ME

How does our
Garden still
Bloom

BUG

Go find
Your Ladybug

A FACT OF LIFE FOR SOME

For some
It is easier to die
Than to discipline
Themselves!

SELF-DESTRUTION

Excessive pleasures
Destroy the life force,
And the instincts debase
The higher aspects
Of the soul.

THE CAREFUL PATH

Just as a mother
Tending her young
Delight always
In self-vigilance

LIBERATION

Before his Liberation
Did some great Bodhisattva
Write love poems from
The Land of the Rising Sun

HEMINGWAY

The Son Also Rises!
The rising Son lights the way!

SOL INVICTUS - THE UNCONQUERED SUN

They shine not in day
They are afraid of the Sun
Stars how cowardly

TO NATURAL BORN WORLD SHAKERS

The road to fame
Is rocky
Like the driveway
To the mailbox

THE WISE

Monks are holy
Artists are talented
Mathematicians are smart
And the wise are disciplined

WHAT THE BUDDHA TAUGHT

In the grip of ignorance
All beings burn with desire
Like the dry fields
Which wither in flame.

A MODERN ZENIC WAY OF TEA

The kettle is hot —
Its sharp whistle told me
The tea woke me

THE PARADOX OF ZEN

How can there be
Happiness without
Emotion

WISDOM FROM THE DHAMMAPADA
ON SELF-CONSTRUCTION

A tranquil mind
Is a happy mind,
So you must strive
For tranquility.

THE GLORIOUS PATH

Transcendental Coincidence
Is the supreme path to
Divine understanding

ENLIGHTENMENT

I began to Know
Without knowing

WISDOM FROM WISDOM TRADITIONS

Goodness is a
Prerequisite
Of greatness.

A MYSTIC'S VIRTUE, AND THE INVISIBLE LABOR OF THOUGHT

To love with the mind
Is a Prophet's profession!

THUNDERBIRD

St. Louis Post-Dispatch
Please keep me Posted.

THE ATMAN

**Dear Lord
I promise
Never to violate
That part of you
Within me**

FAME

People say that,
"You're nobody
Until some
Stranger
Loves
you."

I PLAY DICE WITH THE WORLD

Perhaps, by the grace of God,
I can use the sacred I Ching.

CHAOS THEORY IN PRACTICE

If life is a crap shoot
I want to throw
My own dice!

PHILOSOPHIES GREATEST CONCEPT

Longing for wisdom
Outside the cave of shadows
Plato found the Forms

A MYSTICAL INSIGHT

A glimpse of divine wisdom
By transcendental coincidence
Is easier to acquire than
Wisdom born from meditation

ON PHYSICS AND FRIENDSHIP

Can we measure our sincerity
Without altering it?

CREATION FROM THE NOTHING THAT DIDN'T EXIST

Before the Universe came to be,
There wasn't even any Spacetime;
Like the Zero Dimension
Of an Absolute Singularity.

UNIVERSAL INTERCONNECTEDNESS

The falling of a leaf on earth
Effects every star in the Universe

THE REASON WHY NO EMPIRICAL FORMULA CAN MEASURE LOVE

Math can't measure love
Because love is Transcendental;
Born in that Plane Above
Where Plato was Monumental.

THE HARMONY OF NATURE AND THE LAWS OF PHYSICS

Because Nature is deductive
Physicists can model it by
Mathematical analogy

CON-SCIENCE

Scientists Without a Conscience!

SPIRITUALISM

The Spirit is where
You and God meet.

TO POETS

When the superior one's
Words are exciting -
Read!
When they are dull -
Write!

ON THE SOURCE OF POETRY

Words are from man
Poetry is from God

ON THE GREATNESS OF POETRY

A poor lyric can get by
With a beautiful tune
But a poem has to stand
All alone.

SONGS

Few things can be
More beautiful,
Or more annoying
Than a song!

MYSTICAL POETRY

One mystical poem
Can transcend the
Meaning of a thousand
Pictures because you
Can't take a picture of God
The invisible world
Or the mind

AN INDIAN FAREWELL

Wherever you go in the world,
May your path be one of beauty,
And your destination one of joy!

THE CAUSE OF SO MUCH SUFFERING

The few have
So much wealth,
And such
Great opportunity,
While the many
Have such
Little wealth,
And such
Poor opportunity!

CHILD ABUSE

There are people
Raising children
That shouldn't even
Be allowed to
Raise dogs.

WHAT THEY CANNOT KNOW

A wild flower is like a little
Child that cannot know
How beautiful it is.

EMPATHIC ANALOGY

His puppy fun,
Of tug and tow,
Nip and chew,
And rip,
Lasted till
I took his tail,
And gave it
A little nip!

I AM CERTAIN

You don't need
To read music
To compose a song,
And you don't need
To be a grammarian
To write a poem.

TO THE POLICE, THE FIREMEN, AND THE MILITARY

Greater love has
No one than this,
Than that one
Lay down their life
For strangers.

MY BLESSING FOR YOU

May you always
Walk upon the
Path of greatest joy

BLUEBERRY MOON

THE ESSAY

THE MYSTICAL REFUTATION OF THE GRAND DESIGN

I just read Stephen Hawking's new book called, "The Grand Design," which explains some of the implications of his "Theory of Everything," without going into any of the very complicated mathematics involved in it. After his General Theory of Relativity in 1916, Albert Einstein spent the rest of his life trying to attain the Theory of Everything, but without any success. Einstein called his goal, "The Unified Field Theory." Now Hawking thinks that he has finally accomplished this monumental achievement which he calls "The Grand Design!"

The shocking principle Hawking embraces, is distressing to me, because he believes just like Einstein did, in absolute scientific determinism! Every event, or effect, is predetermined by natural laws, based on these antecedent causes, that could not be otherwise! He carries it so far, that even human thoughts and actions are absolutely contingent on, and governed by, antecedent causes which cannot be otherwise, such that "free will" itself is not possible. Hawking doesn't believe in God or a transcendent realm, and he believes that free will is an illusion, just like Einstein did! Hawking would have us believe, that we are all actors on a stage ignorantly playing out our lives, following a script that has already been written for us by the unconscious laws of nature.

When I was a philosophy student I discovered "The Logical Paradigm," which is the pattern to Aristotle's "Deductive Logic," and at that miraculous time in my life, I fancied myself becoming a logician like Bertrand Russell, and I fell victim to the logic of absolute scientific determinism, and a world without God.

Back in 1905, Einstein wrote a paper called "The Photoelectric Effect" which explained that light is made up of particles he called quanta, and they bump electrons off a zinc plate like billiard balls when light shines on the plate, and this became a foundation stone of great value to Quantum Theory. But Einstein could never come to accept the strange world of subatomic particles, where one discrete particle can exist in more than one place contemporaneously, or especially like the instantaneous action at a distance, between pairs of subatomic particles, defying the "speed of light constant" of Einstein's Special Theory of Relativity, and challenging the fundamental laws of logic. For many years, Niels Bohr discussed this often with Einstein, but he could never get his old friend to accept the strange illogical world of subatomic particles, where God plays dice with the world, just like I learned to do with divination, and the I Ching!

Reverend Dr. John Polkinghorne - a famous Cambridge University particle physicist - wrote that he didn't know why the laws of nature are the way that they are, or why mathematical insight can solve the laws of nature? Now I understand the reason why mathematical insight can solve the laws of nature, and that is simply because nature itself is deductive like the laws of mathematics, and that is why mathematics can model nature in perfect correlation and deductively describe nature! Now my idea sounds like Hawking's scientific determinism, and it sure shakes my religious worldview upside down, and to tell you the truth, the last thing I want to do, is accept it, like I did when I was a student of logic!

Many years after university, my salvation came. I started to believe in God, since it miraculously became my nature to sometimes, mystically acquire wisdom instantly by coincidence, or by deliberation on divine divination. Therefore the only way I could refute Hawking would be with divination, by playing dice, or by waiting for a divine, transcendental coincidence, rather than by refuting Hawking's advanced mathematics, which I am not trained to understand. So let me explain how I refuted "The Grand Design,"

The mystical refutation of "The Grand Design" came as a transcendental coincidence, that my mother and I observed. Now first let me explain my term, "transcendental coincidence." It is a meaningful coincidence, like Carl Jung's term "synchronicity," except that it must occur where the empirical realm and the transcendent realm mystically coincide, or meet in the ecstatic mind of the mystic, but one must wait on it because it comes from the invisible world. So the transcendental coincidence exists as a mystical moment, in which it has been my nature to be absolutely spell-bound, causing a joyful peak-experience, from the new understanding.

Now my dear mom has an absolutely unshakable belief in God and free will, so she wasn't the least bit disturbed by "The Grand Design," but it disturbed me, because I once again, felt the strange seductive power of absolute scientific determinism, like I did as a philosophy student, and I read parts of, "The God Delusion," by Richard Dawkins, and parts of "God Is Not Great," by Christopher Hitchens, and a few of the essays in "The Portable Atheist," and they gave me quite an intellectual beating!

Now not long after I read The Grand Design, and passages from these other books, I was in a paranoid state of anxiety about my faith, and mom and I were talking about this great burden on my mind, and I was praying to myself, as we were driving around, and we came to rest, at a stop sign on North Ridge Road and Hwy 47, and a white van went around the corner in front of us, which read down the side of it, "Free Will Bap." We figured that it meant "Free Will Baptist Church," because there were some letters missing. Well mom in all her tranquil wisdom said, "there you are Kim, there is your answer!" This vision of the white van was not only the answer to my prayer, it was a direct communion with God, by transcendental coincidence about free will. God made it a monumental, mystical experience for us, and an especially sublime one for me. He instantly, startled me, like a Zen master's clout, suddenly enlightening me regarding the truth about Himself, and free will, by granting me and mom, the vision of this white van, with the divine "Free Will" message on it.

HOW TO ORDER BOOKS FROM FERNHOLM PUBLISHING

Check my website: fernholmpublishing.com You will find instructions for ordering books on my website.

Email orders: FernholmP@aol.com

Postal orders: Fernholm Publishing
PO Box 89
Winfield, Missouri, 63389-0089

Sales tax: Please add 6.475% for books shipped to Missouri addresses.

Shipping by air

USA: $ 4.00 for first book add $ 2.00 for each addition book,

Send check or money order made payable to Fernholm Publishing to the address above.

NEW POETRY BOOKS

TITLE: BLUEBERRY MOON
SUB TITLE: THE POEMS & APHORISMS OF KIM LEE SEAGULL
AUTHOR: Kim Lee Seagull
ISBN; 10: 1-883165-72-5
ISBN: 13: 978-1-883165-72-7   LCCN: 2010938385
PRICE: USA $ 19.99

TITLE: WRITTEN ON THE WIND
SUB TITLE: THE POEMS & PROSE OF JUNE HELEN FLEMING:
AUTHOR: June Helen Fleming
ISBN: 10: 1-883165-73-3
ISBN: 13: 978-1-883165-73-4 LCCN: 2010938386
PRICE: USA $ 14.99